The Gazelle

DAVID OLIVER

AMBERLEY

Acknowledgements

Of the many people who have provided a constant stream of information and images, I would like to extend particular thanks to the following individuals and organisations: Christian Da-Silva/Airbus Helicopters, Ian Morris/Airbus Helicopter UK, Geoff Russell/Leonardo Helicopters, ALAT/3 RHC, Craig Davies/The Gazelle Squadron, Jos Stevens/Rotorspot, Aviafora, Patrick Allen, Valentin Edme, Peter Foster, Michael Greenland, Georgina Hunter-Jones, David Nicolle, Alan Norris, Tony Osborne, Dimitrije Ostojic and Francois Prins.

First published 2019

Amberley Publishing
The Hill, Stroud,
Gloucestershire, GL5 4EP

www.amberley-books.com

ISBN 978 1 4456 8868 8 (print)
ISBN 978 1 4456 8869 5 (ebook)

British Library Cataloguing in Publication Data.
A catalogue record for this book is available from the British Library.

Typeset in 11pt on 14pt Celeste.
Origination by Amberley Publishing.
Printed in the UK.

Contents

Introduction

More than fifty years after its maiden flight in France on 7 April 1967, as many as 500 Gazelle helicopters are were still being operated in thirty-four countries, where it is appreciated for its speed, manoeuvrability, ease of maintenance and high degree of reliability.

Developed and manufactured in co-operation with the United Kingdom at the end of the 1960s, and later in the former Yugoslavia and Egypt, more than 1,775 Gazelles have been produced.

The single-engine, five-seat helicopter was a major success in the military sector, with more than 80 per cent of the rotorcraft currently in service being used by armed forces around the world. More than a third of all Gazelles manufactured are still in military service, with the French Army operating more than 100.

A helicopter of many 'firsts', the Gazelle was the first Airbus helicopter to be equipped with the Fenestron, which is still present on Airbus Helicopters light and medium rotorcraft. It was also the first Sud Aviation helicopter to be equipped with glass-resin blades developed in co-operation with the German company Bölkow.

This versatile light helicopter has paved the way for many other technological developments, including viscoelastic dampers, low frequency landing gear and the Non Articulé en Traînée (NAT) main rotor hub.

Lastly, it was the first helicopter in the world to be awarded the IFR qualification Category I by the US Federal Aviation Authority (FAA), allowing operators to fly to instrument flight rules (IFR) with a single pilot on board.

Early interest in the helicopter by the UK led to an Anglo-French development programme under which the Gazelle was produced jointly with Westland Helicopter at Yeovil. The Gazelle was the only helicopters to be adopted by all the UK armed services and would subsequently enter service in the Royal Air Force (RAF) and Royal Navy (RN) in the training role, and the Army Air Corps (AAC) and Royal Marines as a light utility and battlefield reconnaissance helicopter.

Gazelles have been adapted and upgraded with ferry tanks, infrared (IR) signature suppression systems, externally mounted cannon and machine guns with ammunition supplies in the cabin, rescue winches, particle filters for sandy environments, cabin heaters, emergency floatation equipment, high landing skids, engine anti-icing systems and adjustable landing lights. Civilian examples of the Gazelle have been stretched and also equipped with a baggage compartment. Gazelles utilised by law enforcement agencies have been equipped with stabilised camera mounts and lights, along with other specialised surveillance imaging equipment.

Military Gazelles have been upgraded with the latest armament options, 3D navigational displays, electronic flight instrumentation system (EFIS) cockpit displays, night-vision goggle compatibility, ballistic armour packages, direct voice input (DVI) systems for voice control of aircraft systems and advanced autopilot systems.

Ease of maintenance and pilot-friendly operations are hallmarks of the Gazelle. Bearings in the Gazelle are life-rated without the need for continuous application of lubrication. When the helicopter was designed emphasis was placed on minimal maintenance requirements, which translates to low operating costs. Many components in the Gazelle were designed for a 700-hour service life, while some critical components have service lives of up to 1,200 hours before replacement is required.

By 2017, the Gazelle fleet had accumulated more than 7 million flight hours, and it is SA.341 and SA.342 Gazelles that have accumulated the most flight hours, 14,200 and 13,100 respectively, which are currently being flown by civilian operators in the United States.

Sud Aviation's SA.340 Gazelle was flown for the first time on 7 April 1967 from Marignane in the south of France. (Airbus Helicopters)

CHAPTER ONE

Anglo-French Development and Production

Project X.300 was the French state-owned helicopter manufacturer, Sud Aviation's, design to meet the Aviation Légère de l'Armée de Terre (ALAT) requirement for a single-engine light observation helicopter (LOH) to replace the Alouette II in 1966.

Flown for the first time on 7 April 1967 by test pilot Jean Bouet from Marignane in the south of France, the SA.340 Gazelle was powered by a 530-shp (395-kW) Turboméca Astazou IIA turboshaft with transmission from the SA.318C Alouette II combined with a new three-bladed rigid main rotor developed by Bölkow in Germany. It also had a conventional Alouette III tail rotor.

On 12 April 1968, the first Fenestron, invented by Paul Fabre and René Mouille, took to the skies on the second prototype of the Gazelle.

Originally called the Fenestrou, which is Provencal for 'little window', the term evolved into the renowned Fenestron. The idea behind shrouding the tail rotor was initially developed to provide additional safeguards for workers on the ground, but also to protect the tail rotor in forward flight and in complicated operational environments, such as working around high-voltage power lines. Sound reduction benefits followed after much research and optimisation from one generation of Fenestron to the next. The thirteen-blade shrouded anti-torque tail rotor was first certified on the Gazelle in 1972.

The first of four pre-production Gazelles was flown in 1969 and in 1970 Sud Aviation merged with Nord Aviation to form the Aérospatiale Company. Test pilots Denis Prost and Jean-Marie Besse aboard the SA.341 01 F-ZWRH successfully broke three helicopter speed records on 13 May 1971, 3 kilometres at 310 km/h, 15 to 25 kilometres at 312 km/h, and finally the record over 100 kilometres at 296 km/h.

An initial contract for fifty SA.341F Gazelles powered by the 590-shp (440-kW) Astazou IIIA for the ALAT was signed in May 1971 and on 6 August the first official flight of a production Gazelle, SA.341 1001, took place. There are clearly visible differences with the pre-series in the windows of the passenger compartment, the enlarged Fenestron and the repositioned rear winglets, and with the uprated Astazou it had a maximum take-off weight of 1,800 kg.

Early interest from United Kingdom in the Gazelle programme for a common helicopter to equip its three armed forces resulted in an Anglo-French development programme finalised on 22 February 1967, under which Gazelles would be produced jointly by Westland Helicopters in Yeovil and Aérospatiale at Marignane. The agreement allowed the production in the UK of 294 Gazelles and forty-eight SA.330 Pumas ordered by the British Armed Forces, and in return Aérospatiale was given a work share in the manufacturing programme of forty Westland-designed Lynx naval helicopters ordered for the French Navy. Additionally, Westland would have a 65 per cent work share in the manufacturing of the Gazelle and be a joint partner with Aérospatiale on further refinements and upgrades to the helicopter.

Westland evaluated the third pre-production Aérospatiale SA.341 F-ZWRI, which was serialled XW276 in 1969 and the first SA.341B, designated AH.1 for the British Army Air Corps (AAC), XW842, flew on 28 April 1970. The Westland SA.341C Gazelle HT.2 was for the Royal Navy and the SA.341D Gazelle HT.3 and SA.341E Gazelle HCC.4 for the Royal Air Force. The first Westland-built HT.2 of the Royal Navy, XW845, flew on 7 July 1972, while the first HT.3, XW852, flew in the spring of 1973.

The first batch of sixty Westland Gazelles was ordered by the UK Ministry of Defence (MoD) on 21 August 1970 under contract number A23A/1012 (69/71117-02). Built by Westland Helicopters Ltd of Yeovil, they were issued serial numbers XW842 to XW871 and XW884 to XW913. Of this order, twenty-nine were built as Gazelle AH.1s for the AAC, twenty-one as Gazelle HT.2s for the RN and ten for the RAF, nine as HT.3 trainers and one HCC.4 communications/VIP aircraft.

A further eighty-two Westland-built Gazelles were ordered on 9 December 1971 under contract number 70.71082.00 and were serialled XX370 to XX419 and XX431 to XX462. Of this order, sixty-nine were Gazelle AH.1s, nine were Gazelle HT.2s and four were HT.3s.

Order number three was for sixty AH.1s, serial numbers XZ290 to XZ349. A fourth order, KZ/21/34, was placed on 22 October 1976 for thirteen Westland Gazelles, which were to be built at Weston-super-Mare. Serial numbers XZ930 to XZ942 were issued for this batch, of which nine were built as HT.3s and four as Gazelle HT.2s, although only two were delivered to the Royal Navy; the other two aircraft were diverted to the Empire Test Pilots School (ETPS) at Boscombe Down. The penultimate order was for twenty-nine aircraft serialled ZA726 to ZA737, ZA767 to ZA777 and ZA801 to ZA804, comprising twenty-five AH.1s and four HT.3s.

The final order for British military Westland Gazelles were in serial batches ZB625 to ZB629, ZB646 to ZB649 and ZB665 to ZB693, totalling thirty-eight aircraft. Of these twenty-nine were built as Gazelle AH.1s, four as HT.2s and five as HT.3s. The final military Gazelle was AH.1 ZB693, which was delivered to the Army Air Corps in 1983.

New variants that had been coming off the production lines at Marignane included the first military export version, the SA.341H. On 1 October 1971, a licence agreement was signed with the Federal Socialist Republic of Yugoslavia, for 100 SA.341H aircraft to be built by SOKO at its facilities in Mostar. The SA.341G was civil version of the Gazelle powered by the Astazou IIIA derived from the ALAT SA.341F that was issued its French certification on 6 June 1972 and the US FAA certification on 18 September.

For hot and dry military operations, Aérospatiale introduced the SA.342K, powered by the 870-shp (649-kW) Astazou XIVH turboshaft with momentum-separation shrouds over the inlets. First flown on 11 May 1973, the type secured initial sales from Kuwait for a total of twenty aircraft for use in attack and observation roles. Continuing development resulted in a civil version designated SA.342J with an improved Fenestron and higher maximum take-off weight, which was issued French certification on 27 April 1976.

The military counterpart of the SA.342J, the SA.342L, also powered by the Astazou XIVH, was able to carry a wide range of weapons, and more than 100 were subsequently assembled by the Arab British Helicopter Company (ABHC) at Helwan in Egypt. Developed from this version was the more capable SA.342M for the ALAT, which was especially designed for the anti-tank role. Deliveries of 160 SA.342Ms began in 1980.

A long series of trials had been conducted over the years, first with the Gazelle prototype designated SA.349Z and then with its successor, a modified production Gazelle, the SA.349-2 registered F-ZWRN in 1977. With an Astazou XIV engine and stronger transmission and modified main rotor blades, it reached speeds around 186 mph (300 km/hr) and completed a series of flights fitted with small wings designed to explore high manoeuvrability rather than high speed or convertiplane characteristics. The wing produced relatively little lift at high speed but greatly increased the available manoeuvring load factor and its ailerons improved roll rate. The SA.349-2 was also used to collect data on the aerodynamic running of the rotors and the absorption of the vibrations at high speeds.

The SA.342M was the last development of the Gazelle, although a large number of the ALAT aircraft were retrofitted for new weapons systems, sensor and sights. In 1992, Aérospatiale merged its helicopter division with MBB of Germany to form the Eurocopter Group, which would later become part of the European Aerospace & Defense Systems (EADS) group. Later still it became the Airbus Group, with Eurocopter becoming Airbus Helicopter. However, the Gazelle would not remain part of the Eurocopter product line for long, being phased out of production in the mid-1990s after more than 1,560 had been produced in France and Britain.

Sud Aviation SA.340 002 F-ZWRA flew for the first time on 12 April 1968 with the Fenestron ducted tail rotor. (Airbus Helicopters)

Sud Aviation test pilots Rene Mouille and Jean Boulet broke three helicopter records flying SA.341 01 on 13 May 1971. (Airbus Helicopters)

SA.341 1001 F-WTNA, seen flying over central London in 1972. (Airbus Helicopters)

The Gazelle
production line at
Aérospatiale's plant
at Marignane in 1982.
(David Oliver)

Gazelles in final
assembly at
Marignane in 1982.
(David Oliver)

The crowded
assembly shops at
Marignane for SA.341
and SA.342 Gazelles
alongside AS.360
Dauphins in 1982.
(David Oliver)

ALAT SA.342M and Kuwait Air Force SA.342K Gazelles in production at Marignane in 1982. (David Oliver)

Gazelle tail booms in production at Marignane, with SA.330 Pumas in final assembly in the background. (David Oliver)

The experimental winged SA.349-2 used for high-speed trials in 1977 is now in the ALAT Museum at Dax. (ALAT Museum)

Westland Helicopters evaluated the third pre-production Sud-Aviation SA.341, F-ZWRI, which was serialled XW276 in 1969. (Leonardo)

G-BAGJ, the first civil Gazelle produced by Westland Helicopters in 1973, is seen over central London. It is now in the North East Aircraft Museum.

Right: The Westland-built SA.341G Gazelle was fitted with experimental floatation gear in 1973. (Leonardo)

Below: Built in 1974, SA.341G G-BCHM was originally used by the Westland Group, based at Yeovil. (Leonardo)

CHAPTER TWO

In Service with the French Army

A total of 340 Gazelles were procured for the Aviation Légère de l'Armée de Terre (ALAT), 171 SA.341Fs with the Turboméca Astazou IIIC turboshaft, which entered service in 1969, and 161 of the later SA.342M that was a dedicated anti-tank variant with the more powerful Turboméca Astazou XIVH engine.

The SA.341Fs ended up being modified to three different configurations. Sixty-two were converted to support gunships with an SFOM 80 sight and a fixed GIAT M621 20 mm cannon mounted on the left, designated SA.341F/Cannon. Forty were converted to anti-armour gunships with an SFIM optical sight above the cockpit and armed with four HOT anti-tank missiles (ATMs) on pylons, designated SA.341M. They could also be equipped with two rocket launchers for eight SNEB 68 mm EAP unguided rockets. Many of the rest of the SA.341Fs were configured as unarmed scouts with an SFIM M334 Athos sight.

Gazelles could be fitted with an upturned exhaust diffuser to reduce the helicopter's infrared (IR) signature from heat-seeking missiles and sand filters for desert warfare. Some Gazelles were later updated with the advanced composite rotor blades of the Aérospatiale Écureuil helicopter.

The ALAT obtained a variant of the SA.342L that featured an improved Fenestron tail rotor and was powered by the 859-shp (641-kW) Astazou XIVM engine for improved hot and high operations. Designated the SA.342M, it first flew on 11 May 1973. The SA.342M featured a revised instrument panel, a SFIM PA 85G autopilot, Sextant Avionique Nadir self-contained navigation system and Decca 80 Doppler night-flying equipment.

Fitted with an M397 optical sight, the SA.342M could carry up to 1,540 lbs (700 kg) weapons payload that included four or six Euromissile HOT or Aérospatiale AS11 short-range, wired-guided ATMs, 7.62-mm machine guns or a 20-mm GIAT M621 single-barrel revolver cannon mounted on the skids or on external weapons pylons. Up to seventy were upgraded in the 1990s with a SAGEM Viviane stabilised direct view/IR/laser roof-mounted sight to allow night firing of HOT missiles, designated as SA.342M1 Gazelle Viviane. Thirty were retrofitted with the Astazou XIV M2 turboshaft, designated SA.342M ATAMs, and were armed with four Matra/MBDA Mistral air-to-air missiles (AAMs) that were first fired from a Gazelle in 1990 with a Sextant T2000 sight.

By the mid-1980s a number of the Escadrille d'Hélicoptères Légères (EHL) of the ALAT's Régiment d'Hélicopteres Anti-char (RHC) were each fully equipped with ten Gazelles. These included 1 and 2 EHLs of 5 RHC with SA.341F Gazelles for liaison and forward observation based at Pau in the south of France, and 6 RHC with 1 EHL with SA.341F Gazelles and 2 Escadrille d'Hélicoptères Anti-char (EHA) with SA.342M Gazelles with HOT for anti-tank duties based at Compiègne.

Other major units were the Groupes d'Hélicoptères Légères (GHL)s that carried out liaison duties with the Gazelle. These included 11 GHL at Nancy/Essay and 12 GHL at Trier, each with three EHLs equipped, and 13 GHL at Lers Mueaux with one EHL each equipped with ten SA.341F Gazelles

The ALAT training system started at the École de Spécialisation de l'ALAT (ESALAT) at Dax, where SA.341F Gazelles were used for basic training. At the Groupement ALAT de la Section Technique de l'Armée de Terre (GALSTA) at Valence, experienced co-pilots could qualify as captains on the SA.341F. The École d'Application d'ALAT (EAALAT) at Luc/Le Cannet carried out instrument and tactical training with fifteen SA.341F Gazelles, and later SA.342Ms. Smaller Gazelle units included the Escadrille ALAT de l'Armée (EALAT 1A) at Baden-Oos, the Escadrille de la Direction Centrale du Matériel (EDCM) at Bourges and the Escadrille de l'Ergm Alat (EERGM) at Montaubin.

During the Cold War, ALAT regiments were part of larger airmobile units. The 4th Division Aéromobile (4 DAM), which was created in 1985, specialised in airmobile combat within the French Rapid Reaction Force. It was set up to conduct autonomous combat operations and stood ready to engage WARPAC armoured units if they launched an attack on the West from beyond the Iron Curtain.

ALAT SA.341F/SA.342Ms were deployed to Operation *Desert Storm* from 4 DAM/5 RHC with Task Force Alpha based in Saudi Arabia, close to the Iraqi border. As part of the French Operation *Daguet*, the Gazelles supported the French Army during the brief ground phase of the war in February 1991, destroying a number of Iraqi tanks with HOT missiles. The 4 DAM was disbanded in 1995.

In February 1997, Ploče Airfield in Croatia became a French-led Multinational Army Aviation Battalion of Multinational Division – Southeast (MND–SE) of the NATO-led Stabilisation Force in Bosnia and Herzegovina (SFOR). The base operated the French Bataillon de l'Aviation légère de l'Armée de Terre, or BATALAT, with four SA.330 Pumas and four SA.342M/M1 Gazelles until November 2002.

Helicopters from 4 RFHS are frequently deployed to the French Navy's Mistral-class Landing Helicopter Docks (LHDs) as part of a Helicopter Strike Group. Training is focused on all aspects of helicopter operations from an LHD, including low-level navigation over the sea in radio silence and day and night deck landings in all weathers. In 2010 Gazelles from the LHD FS *Tonnerre* deployed to Operation *Atalanta*, the EU anti-piracy operation off the Horn of Africa, fired missiles at a Somali pirate mother ship.

During Operation *Harmattan*, the 2011 Libyan campaign, LHDs FS *Mistral* and *Tonnerre* launched a series of daring ALAT helicopter raids to destroy hostile armour hidden in the desert. Gazelle and Tiger attack helicopters took off for a series of night missions, during which the Gazelles fired 431 HOT anti-tank missiles at a large number of targets, including armoured vehicles and artillery positions.

The annual *Jeanne d'Arc* exercise is a five-month amphibious deployment that takes a French LHD and its Helicopter Strike Group to the Far East, during which the vessel conducts multilateral exercises to develop cooperation and knowledge of this area of deployment. The ports of call provide an opportunity to strengthen defence ties with Djibouti, India, Singapore, Vietnam, China, Japan and Australia during the 24,000-mile (40,800-km) round trip.

The ALAT's permanent DETALAT based in Djibouti fulfils a crucial mission for the projection of the French forces in the Horn of Africa and its helicopters have accumulated more than 90,000 flight hours since 1977. It is currently equipped with four SA.330B Puma helicopters and two SA.342M Gazelle/HOT helicopters. Djibouti is the ideal location for tactical training in a desert environment; the nights are very dark in Djibouti, providing ideal conditions for NVG operations. The DETALAT regularly supports the 5eme Régiment Interarmes d'Outre Mer (5e RIAOM), which is a French marine regiment stationed in Djibouti that carried out joint exercises with the Armée de l'Air 1/88 Corse fighter squadron of Mirage 2000s.

The ALAT's Bataillon Mousquetaire 5 (BATHELICO) is located at the ISAF base at Kabul International Airport in Afghanistan. The battalion was deployed in June 2012 until December 2014 with four Gazelles and four Tigers to undertake ground attack, close combat air support, escort, reconnaissance and overwatch duties. During the deployment, the Gazelles conducted 7,000 flight hours during 5,000 missions and fired some sixty HOT guided missiles in support of ground troops or in the destruction of 'high-value targets', including weapons caches and vehicles.

Operation *Barkhane* was launched in August 2014 as the successor to the French Operation *Serval*, which began in January 2013 against Islamist terrorists in northern Mali with twenty-eight ALAT helicopters, including eight HOT-armed Gazelle Vivianes based at Gao Airport. At the same time the ALAT deployed another four Gazelles and six Pumas out of its base at Bangul in the Central African Republic as part of Operation *Sangaris*. The helicopters in the theatre were used to escort convoys, perform reconnaissance missions and, when necessary, to combine forces with ground troops. The helicopters spend days far away from their home base, moving between locations in the field with the ground troops. France ended this operation in October 2016, while Operation *Barkhane* continued into 2019.

In July 2016, 1, 3 and 5 Régiment d'Hélicoptères de Combat were formed based at Phalsbourg, Étain and Pau respectively and currently operate a total of seven

Escadrilles equipped with Gazelle Vivianes. Also based at Pau is 4 Régiment d'Hélicoptères des Forces Spéciales with one flight equipped with Gazelles. In the field, 4 RHFS aircrews operate in small detachments, each comprising a Gazelle and Puma. Air and ground crew train in all environments – arctic, desert, mountain, jungle and at sea. A Gazelle can deliver a team of two combat swimmers close to a hostile shore or river estuary to carry out undercover reconnaissance and sabotage.

Equipped with twenty-three SA.342M Gazelles, 3 RHS is taking the lead in ALAT Manned-unmanned teaming (MUM-T) trials of chemical, biological, radiological and nuclear operations. In 2018 its aircraft were deployed to the Sahel region of Chad, Mali and Niger, Djibouti and the Republic of Côte d'Ivoire, while its base at Étain is now part of the future CAP HNG 2021 project, which includes opening up to civil and commercial aviation and the renewal of infrastructure, facilities and equipment.

Six of the 3 RHS Gazelles were also modified to carry out trials of a new multi-functional information system, two of which were deployed to the Système d'Information Terminal de l'Aviation Légère de l'Armée de Terre (SIT-ALAT), while another two were deployed to the Central Africa Republic (CAR). A GPS tracker gives a real-time 3D view of the battlefield to the crew of the helicopter, with all the information being displayed on a single screen, giving the patrol leader the position of each of his operational elements and the real-time tactical situation. This information is accessible not only by aircrews but also by the chain of command. Mission planners can customise maps with additional data as the enemy positions, undercover corridors and other strategic elements and all this data can be updated during the mission.

The data can be downloaded for after action reviews (AARs). This modern tool has been designed to be compatible with the next generation of helicopters, as well as the Tiger and the NH90 Caiman, and will be compatible with the new Système d'Information du Combat Scorpion (SICS) that will be one of the main components of the French Army's next generation of land vehicles.

The SIT-ALAT system is the most significant element of the Gazelle's current upgrade programme, which will allow it to remain relevant despite the age of the platform. A total of fifty-eight SA.342M1 and twenty-three SA.342MAs, which are used for crew training and as an airborne sniper platform equipped with the M134 Gatling MiniGun, are being fitted with the SIT-ALAT system. The ALAT is also modernising its Gazelle helicopter fleet to meet the ICAO standards that regulate aviation across the world. As a consequence of the legal aspects of coalition-led operations, they will also receive the Système d'Enregistrement en Vol d'Images Référencées (SEVIR) system, which provides real-time recording of all gun and missile firing actions.

More than 100 SA.342L/M Gazelles remained in ALAT service in 2018, plus another twenty SA.341Fs in secondary roles. They are intended to remain in service for at least another decade before being fully replaced in the scouting and anti-tank missions by the EC665 Tiger HAD and the future light helicopter, the H160M.

Airbus Helicopters is working with the French Ministry of Defence to develop the H160M, which was selected to fulfil a French Armed Forces tri-service requirement for almost 170 rotorcraft. In April 2017, the H160M was selected by France as the basis for its hélicoptère interarmées léger (HIL) programme, which seeks to replace multiple fleets of aged types, including the SA.342 Gazelle, which will be a hard act to follow. A firm contract to officially launch the H160M is expected in 2022, supporting first deliveries after 2025.

One of Aviation Légère de l'Armée de Terre (ALAT) 171 SA.341Fs seen flying over Notre Dame in Paris. (Airbus Helicopters)

A HOT-armed ALAT SA.342M belonging to 2 RHC, based at Allemagne in West Germany, taking part in an exercise in June 1986. (David Oliver)

The Euromissile HOT short-range, wired-guided anti-armour missiles carried by ALAT SA.342M Gazelles in the anti-tank role. (David Oliver)

An ALAT SA.342M seen at Hafar Al Batin on the Saudi–Iraq border during a Gulf War reconnaissance mission in 1991. (ALAT)

An SA.341F at École d'Application d'ALAT (EAALAT) at Luc/Le Cannet in 1984. (David Oliver)

SA.341F Gazelles used for the basic helicopter training at the École de Spécialisation de l'ALAT (ESALAT) at Dax in October 2009. (David Oliver)

An ESALAT SA.341F takes off from Dax Airfield for a training mission in 2009. (David Oliver)

The maintenance hangar for ESALAT SA.341F Gazelles at Dax in 2009, before they were replaced by HeliDax EC120B Colibris. (David Oliver)

More than twenty SA.341F Gazelles remained in ALAT service in secondary roles in 2018. (David Oliver)

HOT-armed SA.342M Gazelles escort an ALAT SA.330B Puma during a tactical training mission from Luc/Le Cannet. (David Oliver)

An SA.342M used for initial firing trials of the Matra/MBDA Mistral air-to-air missile (ATAM) in 1990. (MBDA)

A close formation
of five HOT-armed
SA.342M Gazelles
during a tactical
training exercise
in the south of
France. (ALAT)

An Etain-based
(3 RHC) SA.342M
Gazelle firing a HOT
ATM in 2015. (3 RHC)

An ALAT SA.342M
Viviane Gazelle
aboard the LHD FS
Tonnerre during the
Jeanne d'Arc exercise
off the coast of
Lebanon in 2013.
(David Oliver)

A 4 RHFS SA.342M Gazelle, used for training Special Forces in all environments, is seen during an exercise at Luc/Le Cannet in 2009. (David Oliver)

A crewman firing a six-barrel General Dynamics M-134 MiniGun from a 3 RHC SA.342M1 Gazelle. (ALAT/GAMSTAT)

One of the ALAT's permanent DETALAT SA.342M Gazelles, which are fitted with sand filters and based in Djibouti, in 2015. (David Oliver)

US Marines deliver fuel to a HOT-armed DETALAT SA.342M during a training mission in Djibouti in April 2015. (USMC/ Lance-Corporal Dani A. Zunun)

ALAT Gazelles, fitted with different sand filters, refuel from an ALAT SA.330 Puma in Mali. (ALAT)

A HOT-armed SA.342M Viviane at Sévaré in Mali during Operation *Barkhane* in January 2013. (ALAT)

An SA.342M1 Viviane refuels from a French Army tanker in Mali during Operation *Barkhane* in August 2018. (ALAT)

A 3 RHC SA.342M Viviane painted in a spectacular tiger stripe scheme for the annual NATO Tiger Meet of 2003. (ALAT)

Two 3 RHC SA.342M Gazelles wearing tiger stripes for the 2016 NATO Tiger Meet, which was held at Zaragoza in Spain.

The Night's Watch tiger scheme worn by a 3 RHC SA.342M during the 2017 Tiger Meet at BAN Landivisiau in France. (3 RHC)

A 3 RHC SA.342M Viviane wearing its Bandit Nightmare markings for the 2018 Tiger Meet at Poznań-Krzesiny Air Base in Poland. (3 RHC)

The ALAT Gazelles are due to be replaced by the Airbus Helicopters H160M in 2025 under the hélicoptère interarmées léger (HIL) programme. (Airbus Helicopters)

CHAPTER THREE

The Army Air Corps' 'Whistling Chicken Leg'

Affectionately known by Army Air Corps pilots as the 'Whistling Chicken Leg' and the 'Tinny-Winny', the Westland-built Gazelle AH.1 has been in continuous in service for more than forty-five years.

Three AH.1s were officially accepted to the Gazelle Intensive Flying Trials Unit (IFTU) at Middle Wallop on 3 May 1973. Nine pilots from the three UK services and ten REME technicians spent the next six and a half months clocking up around 2,400 hours of flying.

The IFTU's aircraft included what were among the longest- and shortest-serving Army Air Corps (AAC) Gazelles in terms of time and flying hours. XW850, which was delivered on 2 May 1973, was written off on the 31st of the same month. The cause of the accident, which killed the pilot and injured an aircrewman, was attributed to a jack-stall that happened at low level and at maximum weight. The aircraft crashed at Fordingbridge, Hampshire, and was damaged beyond repair.

XW847 carried out two and a half years of simulated service flying in six months of trials in an effort to find out what was likely to go wrong both from a flying and a maintenance point of view. Each of the three initial AAC helicopters averaged over 100 hours flying per month – a rate of more than three times the average for the army. The main objective of establishing the reliability of the aircraft under typical operating conditions was achieved in a short space of time.

With the job of the IFTU completed, further trials were scheduled with role equipment of various types but at a more normal flying rate, using four aircraft. Personnel and equipment would become part of Demonstration & Trials Squadron (D&T) from December 1973. Preparation for the Gazelle conversion courses was their next main priority. It was envisaged that a one-month conversion course would be necessary for new Gazelle pilots. This would involve around 25 hours in the air plus some extra ground school for those with only piston-engine experience, such as the Westland-built Sioux, which the Gazelle was intended to replace.

The Westland SA.341B first entered operational service on 6 July 1974 with the AAC designated Gazelle AH.1, with No. 660 Squadron based at Salamanca Barracks in West Germany. The five-seat Gazelle AH.1 that replaced the Sioux AH.1 was assigned the roles of reconnaissance, troop deployment, direction of artillery fire, casualty evacuation and anti-tank operations. The AH.1 featured the Astazou IIIN2 engine, a nightsun searchlight and the Decca Doppler 80 Radar, and it could be armed with Raytheon TOW wire-guided anti-tank missiles plus a roof sight. By the mid-1980s the British Army of the Rhine (BAOR) had three armoured regiments on its strength and each division had its own AAC Regiment. 1 Regiment AAC, based at Hildesheim, with Nos 651 and 652 Squadrons, each with eight Lynx AH.1s and four Gazelle AH.1s, operated in the attack/anti-tank roles, while No. 661 Squadron, with twelve Gazelle AH.1s, was a reconnaissance unit. 3 Regiment AAC at Soest had Nos 653 and 662 Squadrons with a mix of Lynx and Gazelle AH.1s and 663 Squadron operating solely Gazelle AH.1s. Finally, 4 Regiment AAC at Detmold had Nos 654 and 659 Squadrons with a mix of Lynx and Gazelles and No. 669 Squadron with only Gazelle AH.1s. A small number of Gazelles were operated by 664 Squadron at Minden as the BAOR Communications Flight while No. 12 Flight was based at RAF Wildenrath for communications duties.

No. 7 Flight AAC was based at RAF Gatow in West Berlin in the 1980s. Directly under the control of the Berlin Brigade the main task of this small unit comprising three Gazelle AH.1s was that of the Berlin Wall surveillance and daily observation of the 55,000 Soviet troops based within sight of Gatow. Its secondary duties included VIP and military personnel transport, as well as support of the West German police, which was not permitted to operate its own helicopters over the city.

24 (Airmobile) Brigade was formed on 1 April 1987 at Catterick, North Yorkshire, as one of the BAOR reinforcing brigades to provide the NATO Northern Army Group (NORTHAG) with an effective counter to massed enemy armoured movements. Gazelle AH.1s of all front line units assigned to the brigade were equipped with the Ferranti AF532 observation aid. During its predominantly Cold War service period in West Germany, AAC Gazelles flew over 660,000 hours and had over 1,000 modifications made to the aircraft.

UK-based AH.1 units included No. 6 Flight, part of No. 658 Squadron at Netheravon, No. 657 Squadron at Oakington and No. 655 Squadron at Belfast-Aldergrove, along with a detachment at Ballykelly with No. 656 Squadron. The type was also frequently used to perform airborne patrols in Northern Ireland as part of Operation *Banner*, the British Armed Forces' operation in Northern Ireland from August 1969 to July 2007.

On 17 February 1978, Gazelle AH.1 XX404 of No. 657 Squadron crashed near Jonesborough, County Armagh, after coming under fire from the Provisional IRA during a ground skirmish, killing one of the crew. An active service unit of the Provisional IRA shot down Gazelle AH.1 ZB687 on 11 February 1990 along the border between Northern Ireland and the Republic of Ireland. The helicopter was hit several times by heavy machine-gun fire and crash-landed on an open field, injuring three members of its four-man crew.

Another Gazelle AH.1 was written-off in Northern Ireland on 27 November 1992 when ZB681 of No. 661 Squadron was involved in a mid-air collision with an RAF Puma on approach to RAF Aldergrove. Both the helicopters crashed, killing all four on board the Puma and the two on board the Gazelle seriously injured.

The first overseas deployment outside of the British Isles and Europe began in 1974 when AAC Gazelle AH.1s replaced Sioux helicopters operated by No. 660 Squadron at RAF Sek Kong. However, they were found to be unsuitable for Hong Kong operations and by the end of 1975 had been replaced by the Westland Scout AH.1.

Operation *Agila* took place in Rhodesia, later Zimbabwe, in the lead up to the country's first free elections in 1980, leading to independence from British rule. To assist with this process, six Gazelle AH.1s of No. 656 Squadron supported the 1,500-strong Commonwealth Monitoring Group (CMG) tasked with setting up of rendezvous and assembly points prior to the ceasefire and in preparation for the subsequent elections. The ceasefire between the various guerrilla groups officially began at 00:01 on 29 December 1979, although reports of intimidation tactics and threats of violence would continue to mar the election process. Operation *Agila* coincided with the wet season in Rhodesia, the results being that regular heavy tropical thunderstorms led to the sporadic grounding of No. 656 Squadron throughout the months they served. Tasks undertaken by the Gazelles involved the movement of men, materiel and supplies, as well as liaison sorties for senior members of CMG staff and the Rhodesian Patriotic Front Headquarters. When necessary, the helicopters were employed in CASEVAC duties for the wounded of both the CMG and Rhodesian forces.

Other overseas AAC Gazelle AH.1 units in the mid-1980s included No. 25 Flight based at Belize International Airport for support and communication duties and No. 29 Flight at Suffield, Canada, with five AH.1s in support of British Army Training Unit Suffield (BATUS) delivering CASEVAC, range safety control and C2, plus ISTAR support to the formations in training. From 1988 to September 1994, the AAC United Nations Peacekeeping Force in Cyprus (UNFICYP) Flight was equipped with Gazelle AH.1s.

Army-owned AH.1s also entered service with 3 Commando Brigade Air Squadron (3 CBAS), where they operated as utility and reconnaissance helicopters in support of the Royal Marines based at RNAS Yeovilton. The twelve Gazelles for

3 CBAS had entered service in 1975. The unit was a self-sufficient light helicopter squadron tasked with supporting 3 Commando Brigade worldwide. It consisted of four flights – two equipped with four AH.1s for observation, forward air control (FAC), liaison and CASEVAC, one of six TOW-equipped Lynx AH.1s and a HQ flight responsible for administration and tasking. All the aircraft were maintained by REME personnel attached to the squadron. Three 3 CBAS AH.1s were stationed at St George's Barracks in Malta during 1977. During the Falklands War, the 3 CBAS Gazelles played a valuable role operating from the flight decks of Royal Navy ships. Under a rapidly performed programme specifically for the Falklands operation, the Gazelles were fitted with 68-mm SNEB rocket pods and various other optional equipment such as IFF, armour, flotation gear and folding blade mechanisms. A total of fifteen Gazelles were sent to the South Atlantic in 1982 flown by Royal Marines and two were lost on the first day of the landings at San Carlos Water. On 21 May two CBAS AH.1s, XX402 and XX411, were escorting RN Sea King HC4s when they were shot down near Port San Carlos by small arms fire from retreating Argentine troops, and a third, XX412, was badly damaged. From then on most shore-based Gazelles were confined to CASEVAC and support roles to minimise contact with the enemy.

However, in a high-profile incident of friendly fire on 6 June 1982, a Gazelle AH.1 was mistaken for a low-flying Argentine C-130 Hercules and was shot down by a British Type 42 destroyer. Gazelle AH.1 XX377 was originally on the strength of 3 CBAS but was allocated to No. 656 Squadron on sailing for the Falklands aboard *Nordic Ferry* on 9 May. It arrived at San Carlos on 3 June and three days later it was tasked to take spares and fuel from Darwin to Mount Pleasant. While some 2 miles from the peak, flying at between 70 and 200 feet AGL in bad weather and poor visibility, the Gazelle was hit by a Sea Dart missile fired from the destroyer HMS *Cardiff*.

The Gazelle crashed immediately and was destroyed. All four occupants were killed on impact. HMS *Cardiff* was reported to have fired two Sea Darts early on 6 June at unidentified and slow-moving aircraft heading east towards Fitzroy settlement, but no hits were confirmed. The destroyer's commander had been told that the target was in an area where no 'friendly' aircraft were operating. On 13 June another casualty of the raid on 3 Commando Brigade's HQ by Argentine Skyhawks was Gazelle ZA728, which had its Perspex bubble canopy shattered. The aircraft was recovered to the rear echelon at San Carlos for repairs, but as the Gazelle had also suffered serious damage to the instrument panel it was decommissioned.

With over thirty years of air experience, Lt-Com. Bill O'Brien RM was awarded the Distinguished Flying Medal (DFM) while flying a Gazelle at the battles of Darwin and Goose Green. His work in Operation *Corporate* involved rescuing casualties and delivering supplies.

'We flew a number of sorties mostly at night in an armed Gazelle, not that we ever used the SNEB 68 mm rockets in anger,' he said. 'I am not sure how effective they would have been if we had – they had a fairly basic aiming system just a chinagraph cross on the aircraft windscreen. It was the early days of night vision devices. They were fairly rudimentary and we taught ourselves how to use them on the way down to the South Atlantic.'

However, AAC Gazelles would not leave the Falkland Islands until five years after the Falklands conflict came to an end. The AAC Falkland Island Squadron operated a flight of Gazelle AH.1s based at Port Stanley Airport until Mount Pleasant Airbase was opened in 1987.

Tasked with communications and VIP flights plus some coastal reconnaissance, which included deck-landing practice on Royal Navy ships on patrol, a technique not taught at Middle Wallop, the Gazelles were expected to operate year round in the challenging weather conditions of the Falklands at their wind, weight and endurance limits. This service was commonly referred to by army personnel as 'TITS', being the acronym for 'The Inter-island Taxi Service'.

The first full AAC regiment was shipped out to the Gulf in January 1991 as part of Operation *Grapple*, comprising twenty-four Gazelle AH.1 and twenty-four Lynx AH.7 helicopters of 4 Regiment and drawn from Nos 654, 659 and 661 Squadrons. The Gazelles were already fitted with sand filters and painted in desert 'pink' camouflage. Normally unarmed, the AAC Gazelles were also fitted with unguided rocket pods when deployed to Operation *Desert Sabre,* the ground campaign of the Gulf War in February 1991.

Operation *Haven* was the UK's contribution to Operation *Provide Comfort*, a multi-national effort to provide protection and humanitarian aid to Kurdish refugees fleeing oppression by Saddam Hussein's forces after the Gulf War. Royal Marines from 40 and 45 Commando and other 3 Commando Brigade elements were involved in the operation in April 1991, supported by four 3 CBAS AH.1s deployed to Task Force *Bravo*.

Following the end of the Cold War at the end of 1991, the structure of BAOR changed and with the end of the Warsaw Pact British Forces began plan a withdrawal from Germany but AAC Gazelles were soon fully deployed to operations far from Europe.

In 2000 AAC Gazelle AH.1s flew overhead spotting for mortar teams as they pounded rebel forces in support of the SAS rescue mission in Sierra Leone during Operation *Barras*, while 3 CBAS Gazelles supported Operation *Telic,* the UK military operations in Iraq from 2003. In 2007, it was reported that, while many British helicopters had struggled with the conditions of the Afghani and Iraqi theatres, the Gazelle was the best performing aircraft, with roughly 80 per cent being available for planned operations.

During pre-Operation *Herrick* exercises, a crucial asset that battle groups called on when in Helmand was Intelligence, Surveillance, Target Acquisition and Reconnaissance (ISTAR), and an important part of that was the use of unmanned aerial vehicle (UAV) surveillance. However, as UAVs are not licenced to fly in UK airspace; instead, that role was taken by a Gazelle AH.1 equipped with an MX-15 EO/IR sensor turret.

The Gazelle has also been used by Middle Wallop-based Army Air Corps helicopter aerobatic teams, including the Blue Eagles originally formed in 1973 with five Sioux AH.1s and briefly reformed in 1982 as the Silver Eagles for the AAC's 25th anniversary with Gazelles. The team was re-configured in 1992 with four Gazelles and a single Lynx. The Sparrowhawks was another four-Gazelle aerobatic team that displayed in 1977.

AAC AH.1s were upgraded in 2007 with a Direct Voice Input (DVI) system developed by QinetiQ that allows the aircrew to control aircraft systems using voice commands and access information without removing their hands from the flight controls or their eyes from the outside world.

In 2016 the Service Modifications team at No. 1710 Naval Air Squadron (NAS) developed a system for the AAC Gazelle AH.1 to be adapted to airlift casualties from the battlefield. Each year the army deploys to the British Army Training Unit Suffield (BATUS) in Alberta, Canada, for live firing exercises, but needed to provide a helicopter medical evacuation facility to cover the large prairie of 1,042 square miles. The design team introduced life-monitoring and life-support equipment normally found in a UK air ambulance as part of the modifications and trialled their designs with No. 667 Squadron.

At the beginning of 2018, ten Gazelle AH.1s remained in service with No. 665 Squadron, 5 Regiment in Northern Ireland, plus six with No. 7 Regiment Conversion Flight at the School of Army Aviation at Middle Wallop, where the Gazelle has been used to train AAC pilots for the past forty-five years, and No. 667 Squadron. Four more continued to serve with No. 29 Flight BATUS in Canada, while another ten AH.1 remained at Middle Wallop, undergoing servicing or in storage.

Although the original Gazelle out of service date (OSD) was set in 2018, Gama Engineering Ltd, at Fairoaks Airport, was awarded a contract in April 2017 to supply the design solution and major parts for a Traffic Alerting System, GPS and 8.33 kHz VHF communications upgrade and a Primary Flight Display from Aspen Avionics to a number of AAC Gazelle AH.1s. In March 2018 Vector Aerospace was awarded a contract to provide maintenance support for the AAC Gazelle AH.1 helicopter fleet at its Fleetlands facility in Gosport. Work under the contract commenced in April 2018, and with Contract Extension Options will continue until 30 June 2022.

Although the British Army plans to replace the Gazelle with a new type by 2025, none was selected by the end of 2018 and it is likely that the venerable Army Air Corps' 'Whistling Chicken Leg' will remain beyond its 50th anniversary in UK military service.

Gazelle AH.1 XW847 was one of three Gazelles assigned to the Intensive Flying Trials Unit (IFTU) at Middle Wallop in May 1973, flying over 100 hours per month. (Francois Prins)

Gazelle AH.1 of 665 Squadron deployed to Rhodesia in 1979 as part of Operation *Agila*. (665 Squadron)

Delivered to the AAC in 1977, AH.1 XZ316 was used for pilot training with 670 Squadron at Middle Wallop. (David Oliver)

Left: AH.1 XX403 was one of the five Gazelles in the Silver Eagles aerobatic team in 1982. (Patrick Allen)

Below: A gathering of 670 Squadron Gazelle AH.1s at Middle Wallop in 1984, with XZ332, built in 1977, in the foreground. (Alan Norris)

Gazelle AH.1 XX386 of 12 Flight, a reconnaissance unit based Hildenheim, West Germany, lifts off from RAF Wildenrath in 1984. (David Oliver)

Gazelle AH.1 ZA735 was one of two equipped with floatation gear that were assigned to 25 Flight, based in Belize, in 1985. (David Oliver)

670 Squadron AH.1 XX457 crashed at Middle Wallop on 23 October 1987 during a sloping ground-landing exercise. Fortunately there were no casualties. (Crown Copyright)

AH.1 XZ294 from 663 Squadron, based at Soest, carried referees during Exercise *Lionheart* in West Germany in 1984. (David Oliver)

Gatow-based 7 Flight Gazelle AH.1 XX386 formates with the Soviet Mi-8 Hip during a Berlin Wall surveillance flight in 1988. (7 Flight)

Gazelle AH.1 XX404 of 657 Squadron was shot down by IRA small fire while on Northern Ireland border patrol on 11 February 1990. (Crispin Rodwell)

664 Squadron Gazelle AH.1 XZ347, wearing the desert pink scheme it wore during Operation *Grapple* in the 1991 Gulf War. (Patrick Allen)

Army Air Corps Gazelle AH.1s undergoing maintenance at the Royal Naval Air Yard (RNAY) Fleetlands in 1992. (Francois Prins)

Impressive aerobatics by the reformed Blue Eagles team of four Gazelle AH.1s and a Lynx in 1992. (Alan Norris)

From 1988 to September 1994, the AAC UNFICYP Flight in Cyprus was equipped with unmarked Gazelle AH.1s. (Patrick Allen)

670 Flight Gazelle AH.1 ZA769 formating with an AAC Lynx AH.7 over the Salisbury Plain Training Area in 1994. (Patrick Allen)

Right: AAC Gazelle AH.1 helicopters carrying trainee forward air controllers (FACs) at RAF Spadeadam, Cumbria, in October 2004. (Crown Copyright)

Below: AH.1 ZA766 of 671 Squadron was part of the British Team Helicopter Championships at Netheravon in 2004. (Alan Norris)

Two Gazelle AH.1s and a single Lynx AH.1 of the Blue Eagles aerobatic team at the Royal International Air Tattoo (RIAT) in 2005.

654 Squadron AH.1 XX449 in Northern Norway during Exercise *Clockwork* in November 2007. (David Oliver)

AH.1 XZ349 was used to train Afghani Mi-17 pilots at Boscombe Down as part of Team *Active* in 2010. (David Oliver)

AH.1 ZB686, equipped with a NightSun and MX-15 sensor for operation in Northern Ireland, was later to act as a UAV in pre-Afghan deployment exercises. (Patrick Allen)

AH.1 XW865 was assigned to 29 Flight at Suffield, Canada, in support of British Army Training Unit Suffield (BATUS) in 2011. (Crown Copyright)

A BATUS AH.1 taking part in an exercise with the Georgia National Guard's UH.60 Black Hawk in September 2012. (US Army)

On board BATUS AH.1 XZ340 during an exercise with the Georgia National Guard in Atlanta in 2012. (US Army)

3 Commando Brigade Air Squadron (3 CBAS) Gazelle AH.1 XX376 with an AAC Scout AH.1 in Norway in 1980. (RM)

Following early losses in the Falklands Conflict, 3 CBAS Gazelle AH.1s were used for casualty evacuation (CASVAC) missions. (RM)

Above: 3 CBAS Gazelle AH.1 ZA776 in the Falklands in May 1982 was fitted with SNEB 68-mm rockets, which were never used. (RM)

Right: A 3 CBAS Gazelle AH.1 fitted with floatation gear when taking part in Exercise *Clockwork* 1989 off the coast of Norway. (Patrick Allen)

Four 3 CBAS AH.1s took part in Operation *Haven* to protect Kurdish refugees following the Gulf War in April 1991. (Patrick Allen)

Wearing the Union Flag, 3 CBAS AH.1 ZA728 participated in Operation *Haven* on the borders of Turkey and Iraq. (Patrick Allen)

AH.1 XX380 of 3 CBAS takes off from Camp Justice on Masirah Island, Oman, during Operation *Enduring Freedom* in 2002. (USAF)

3 CBAS AH.1 XX399 flying over Norway wearing skis on the landing skids during Exercise *Clockwork* 2006. (Patrick Allen)

CHAPTER FOUR

Royal Air Force Service

The first of thirty-two Westland-built Royal Air Force (RAF) SA.341Cs, designated Gazelle HT.3s, was delivered to Training Command on 17 July 1973 and entered service with the Central Flying School (CFS) at RAF Ternhill in Shropshire in August 1974, replacing the Westland-built Sioux. The rotary-wing element of the CFS moved to No. 2 Flying Training School (FTS) at RAF Shawbury in September 1976 when Ternhill closed. The training fleet then comprised Gazelle HT.3s pooled with No. 1 Squadron or the CFS as required. The unit at RAF Shawbury was seen by many as the premier helicopter training unit worldwide and consequently not only trained pilots from the UK, but also from many other air arms.

During the 1980s, after completing a course with the Elementary Flying Training Squadron (EFTS) at RAF Swinderby on fixed-wing Chipmunks, and a 40-hour basic flying training on the Tucano, RAF students streamed for helicopters were posted to Shawbury to begin an demanding eighteen-week training course.

Apart from this course there were also a variety of other short courses, such as a four-week refresher training course and a four-week staff conversion course. Even RAF Harrier pilots were sent to RAF Shawbury for a one-week course essentially designed to get them used to hovering as they had had no experience of this particular manoeuvre during their fixed-wing fast jet training.

All the student pilots started with ground school, which could last for anything from one to four weeks depending on the course, and this was helped considerably by recently introduced cockpit procedures trainers (CPTs). The ground phase was followed by a further four to five weeks, during which the student pilot was introduced to flying the helicopter for the first time and got to grips with basic flying techniques and handling qualities that were quite different to a fixed-wing aircraft.

The remainder of the course consisted of applied flying with training in all aspects of helicopter operations, including navigation, low-level flying, landing in confined clearings, underslung load operations, search and rescue training, engine-off landings, autorotations and night flying. The training schedule was designed to keep students on their toes and as soon as they had mastered one aspect of flying they moved rapidly on to the next phase. As the training progressed there was a certain amount of role-reversal, with the student playing the part of the instructor and vice versa. Towards the end of the course the students were streamed for operational training on a Sea King, Puma or Chinook.

Ian Morris, head of defence business at Airbus Helicopters UK, has fond memories of the Gazelle:

As former Nimrod aircrew I was completing training on the Jet Provost at RAF Linton-on-Ouze when a colleague dropped in and gave me a flight in one of the RAF's new Gazelle helicopters. I was hooked and transferred to RAF Shawbury where the Gazelle was based for helicopter pilot training in 1979 with No. 1 Squadron. I was on the second Gazelle course, and completed the 80-hour basic helicopter training course after which I completed advanced training on the Wessex before being posted to RAF Valley for a 15-hour Search and Rescue (SAR) course on the Whirlwind before converting to the Puma.

In 1984 I returned to Shawbury for a 50-hour CFS(H) helicopter instructor's course on the Gazelle and then went on to instruct on No. 1 Squadron for three years. The Gazelle was a very good modern helicopter that got better as time went on. It used to fly fast and although it had no navigation aids, other than clock and compass, it was a good grounding for the latest RAF types, the Puma and Chinook. It had very few vices and was fitted with a Fenestron as a tail rotor, which made things much safer especially in the event of a tail rotor failure, where, for the first time if the speed was kept up to 40 knots one could make a running landing under power rather than an engine off landing.

I was a Gazelle display pilot for a couple of seasons with a standard routine that exploited the best of the aircrafts attributes. It was easy to display and to keep it within sight of spectators especially at non-airfield venues. We also dropped into local recruiting events at fetes and country fairs around the country to give people a close up view of a modern RAF aircraft. We were also invited to take part in a number of school visits.

The Gazelles at Shawbury also had a war role to play. Aircraft with a pilot and observer would regularly deploy to operational bases in West Germany during exercises. We would position close to the airfields that were under simulated attacks and carry out airfield repair reconnaissance reporting the condition of the runways and facilities to see if the airfield could remain operational.

Overall the Gazelle was a fun aircraft to fly and a good instructional aircraft and it came as no surprise to many who had flown it that when the time came for it to be replaced, its larger brother the Squirrel was selected.

Ian has continued his connection with the Gazelle as Airbus Helicopter UK has an MOD contract to provide technical support and logistics to the Army Air Corps extant Gazelle fleet.

One of the 2 FTS Gazelle HT.3s was the first RAF aircraft to be finished in an experimental olive green drab scheme in 1989, but this was not adopted as standard and it reverted to its normal red and white scheme during its next scheduled respray.

A few Gazelle HT.3s were converted as SA.341E to serve as short-range communications aircraft and supplied to No. 32 Squadron based at RAF Northolt. Designated Gazelle HCC.4s, they provided short-range light communication and fast VIP transport duties. Northolt is directly beneath one of the London heli-routes, and while the Gazelles have no problems flying directly out of the Zone to the north, they required Heathrow clearance to fly south, usually via Battersea. No. 32 Squadron's four Gazelle HCC.4s differed little from that of the HT.3 trainers at RAF Shawbury, although they were fitted with additional radios, a radio altimeter and more comfortable seats. All flights were VFR and averaged no more than a 50-mile radius. Once a year they deployed to West Germany to exercise with troops in their war role of observation and liaison.

One of the Gazelle HCC.4s, XW855, was withdrawn from service on 2 April 1996 after a total flying time of 3,958 hours. Stored initially at RAF Shawbury, it was moved to RAF Museum Hendon in April 2003, where it remains on display.

After its RAF retirement the Gazelle has continued to be used for testing and trials. The Rotary Wing Test & Evaluation Squadron (RWTES) is a tri-service UK military organisation based at MoD Boscombe Down in Wiltshire. Primarily, the squadron is responsible for test and evaluation of rotary wing aircraft and equipment, or their associated modifications. It role is to test and evaluate rotary wing aircraft and their associated equipment and weapon systems to generate evidence to support recommendations for Military Aircraft Release/Release To Service.

The RWTES was part of the Defence Evaluation & Research Agency (DERA) until 2 July 2001, when it became a part of RAF Strike Command, now Air Command, working in a public-private partnering arrangement with QinetiQ. All of its test pilots are graduates of the Empire Test Pilots School (ETPS), also located at MOD Boscombe Down.

RWTES has used four Gazelles permanently based at Boscombe Down, the longest serving of which is the former RAF Gazelle HT.3 XZ936. Commissioned in May 1978, it lived its entire life at Boscombe Down, until it was damaged in an accident in 2014. Two other Gazelles, former RN HT.2 XZ939 and former RAF HT.3 ZB625, were used for continuation training and trials work as well for instruction use by ETPS. They are due to be replaced by four Airbus Helicopter H125s in 2019.

Four Gazelle HT.3s in service with the Central Flying School (CFS) at RAF Ternhill in 1974. (CFS)

Gazelle HT.3 XW858, belonging to No. 1 Squadron of No. 2 Flying Training School (FTS), is seen at RAF St Mawgan in 1974. (Training Command)

A pair of No 2 FTS Gazelle HT.3s taking part in a flying display at RAF Waterbeach in September 1977. (David Oliver)

Gazelle HT.3s of No. 1 Squadron of No. 2 FTS, XW862 and XX406, are seen on the apron of RAF Shawbury in September 1981. (David Oliver)

No. 2 FTS Gazelle HT.3 XZ937 on a low-level training sortie over the Shropshire countryside in 1981. (David Oliver)

A No. 2 FTS Gazelle HT.3 using a confined space helipad near RAF Shawbury in 1981. (David Oliver)

No. 2 FTS Gazelle HT.3 XW906 was eventually delivered to Qinetiq for apprentice training in 2011. (David Oliver)

No. 1 Squadron Gazelle HT.3 XZ931, seen lifting off from RAF Shawbury in 1981, is now on the South African civil register. (2 FTS)

2 FTS HT.3 ZB267 was the first RAF aircraft to be finished in an experimental olive green drab scheme, in 1989, but it later reverted to its normal red and white scheme. (Patrick Allen)

2 FTS Gazelle HT.3 ZA803, seen lifting off from Locking in March 1989, was later sold the Congo Democratic Republic after being withdrawn from RAF service in 1997. (David Oliver)

Gazelle HT.3 XW855 was modified into an HCC.4 VIP transport in 1978 and is now on display at RAF Museum Hendon. (Alan Norris)

Former RN Gazelle HT.2 XZ939 entered service with the Empire Test Pilots School (ETPS) at MOD Boscombe Down in 1992. (Tony Osborne)

'Tester 3', a former AAC Gazelle AH.1, XX453, was operated by Qinetiq and flown by ETPS student pilots. (QinetiQ)

Former RAF HT.3 ZB625 transferred to QinetiQ in 2010 and operated in the Salisbury Plain Training Area (SPTA). (Tony Osborne)

On board Qinetiq Gazelle HT.3 XZ936 'Tester 73' during a ceiling exercise by ETPS pilots in 2012. (Qinetiq)

Another former AAC AH.1, XX449 joined Qinetiq's fleet of trials aircraft in 2010. It is seen here over SPTA with an RAF Chinook. (Qinetiq)

Chapter Five

The Gazelle Joins
the Senior Service

The Royal Navy's Gazelle HT.2 entered service in March 1974 with No. 705 Naval Air Squadron (NAS) at RNAS Culdrose to provide all-through flying training in preparation for the Lynx's service entry. A total of twenty-three Gazelles were ordered for the Culdrose unit, which was the basic training unit for RN helicopter pilots. The only difference from the RAF HT.3 was that the HT.2 had a rescue hoist. HT.2 student pilots under training were drawn from the General of Supplementary Lists of the Naval Officer Corps. Their previous flying experience included 10 hours of aptitude flying in fixed-wing Chipmunks of the Naval Flying Grading Flight based at Roborough, Plymouth, and a 60-hour Elementary Flying course on Bulldogs at RAF Topcliffe in Yorkshire.

One of the student pilots was Cdr Michael Greenland MVO:

My introduction to the Gazelle was in July 1983. I had just turned nineteen and was a Midshipman in the RN and midway through the RN Flying Training pipeline. The Falklands War had finished the previous year and the Navy was running an accelerated Flying Training Programme to rebuild their pilot numbers.

I had completed my Final Handling Test from Topcliffe, on the Bulldog T.1 on 1 July, graduated from RN Elementary Flying Training and driven down to join No. 705 Naval Air Squadron at RNAS Culdrose to start Basic Flying Training where I completed my Gazelle and area familiarisation on 22 July.

My memories of the Gazelle, and my experience learning to fly helicopters are entirely positive. Relatively basic, the HT.2 had a simple hydraulic system, which could be switched off for practice, a straightforward flying control interlink design to introduce an element of automatic inputs in other controls when one made an input in, say, the collective. It included a very modest Stability Augmentation System (SAS) and trim to reduce the need for constant control corrections to stay in a stable hover or straight and level flight. The Astazou gas turbine was simple to start and operate, with no twist throttle requirements.

A brilliant, innovative Fenestron tail design, and incredibly advanced design for its time I came to love the Gazelle its name being amazingly apt. Compared to fixed wing trainers and subsequent frontline helicopters it had unnerving all round visibility and therefore one felt a true sense of being in the air. With the enormous benefit that, in the light training role, it had plenty of spare power, was highly agile and fast while being most forgiving of errors. Being simple, easy to maintain and with an unfussy, small and highly reliable engine it was fantastic for the staff and students that we could run an 18 line flying programme all day out of a pool of just over twenty aircraft.

Looking back, from the pilots perspective as a training helicopter it was superb. Learning to hover, it ensured you had to develop rotary coordination skills, as you raised the collective it did try to turn and pitch so you had to move the pedals and cyclic to keep it pointing in the right direction and in a steady hover. Of course the QHI would often make you practice without the SAS so you really had to work hard and prove your skill. Just occasionally they would also fail the trim or hydraulics to ensure you really were concentrating, and could deal with an emergency. Without hydraulics the Gazelle really is very heavy and only just controllable. Aloft it was a dream, excellent visibility and limited instrumentation meant navigation was true clock, map ground.

Culdrose, being in south west Cornwall and therefore never far from the sea, had its advantages in terms of navigation, however we would just fly up to North Devon low level where the terrain had remarkably few unique features for the young pilot to hang his hat on. Landing was equally challenging as it danced around as the ground effect increased with the requirement to land in a small circle.

The Gazelle was a fantastic helicopter to learn low level skills. With such good all round visibility you could practice from 50 to 500 feet, flying up to 120 kts, with excellent agility and manoeuvrability you really felt you were at one with the aircraft and the environment around you. You had the spare power to practice transitions into and from the smallest of confined areas which was ideal for the student pilot to get to grips with all the different approach and departure techniques. Being skidded ensured you could land in fairly unprepared surfaces albeit one did not wish to bend an aerial or dent the belly.

Running landings up to 30 kts were always interesting as one felt alarmingly close to the ground and yet were still a few feet up! Similarly, care was needed on sloping grounds with slopes up to 10 degrees being broadly possible. Engine off landings (EOLs) were also taught and, while challenging for all concerned never practiced solo. Much effort was put in to ensure we did not overdo it with the QHI always poised to intervene if we did not get it absolutely right.

705 NAS also introduced us to instrument flying (IF). A helmet visor and velcro screens did their best to hide the horizon and outside world and to try to focus your attention on the small analogue instruments located on a central instrument panel. A basic Attitude Indicator, Altitude, Airspeed, Rate of Climb and Descent Indicators were all laid out for a basic T shaped scan, with just the Torque Meter and T's and P's down and off to one side. We were soon introduced to 'actual' and I recall spending many a flight practicing climbing and descending coordinated turns.

There are of course a number of vices and 'gotchas' with the Gazelle. Like many helicopters you could over torque it and lose control moving sideways or turning too fast in the hover in gusty wind conditions. In the 705 NAS training environment we were shown these but not, allowed to fly in weather conditions that made these a likely occurrence. In a well-run professional training environment the risks and likelihood of accidents can be minimised.

Finishing off with basic helicopter close formation my Course and early time with the Gazelle completed after six months and near 95 hours day and night. I gained my Wings and was quickly moved on to the much more complex Sea King HAS.2. It was only then that you realised what fun the Gazelle really is. In my view it is a true pilot's helicopter, light, simple, responsive and fast; free from the strictures of weight and complexity. A true delight to fly.

The Sharks

The Sharks were the Royal Navy's helicopter display team, flying Gazelle HT.2 helicopters. The team was formed in 1975 from No. 705 NAS, based at RNAS Culdrose, Cornwall. Made up of six helicopters, all six pilots were instructors and trained formation aerobatics in their spare time. Painted red, white and grey with a shark emblem on the tail fin, they were equipped with orange and green smoke canisters fitted to the skis.

After two successful seasons, during which time the Sharks built up a well-deserved reputation for their entertaining close-formation routines and thoroughly professional displays, flying only a quarter of a rotor diameter apart, well into the 1977 season it was preparing for an appearance at the Queen's Jubilee review of the fleet at Spithead.

On 13 June the team took off from Culdrose for a full practice of its display routine. In good weather and clear visibility the team began their formation practice a mile offshore over Mounts Bay. During a turn, Nos 4 and 6 aircraft collided, suffering fatal damage and crashing into the sea. No. 1 aircraft, flown by Team Leader Lt-Com. Alan Rock, was severely damaged in the collision but was able to make an emergency landing in a field on a nearby clifftop, where he and his passenger were treated for shock.

Within minutes of the accident, two Sea King and Wessex helicopters from Culdrose arrived over the scene and two lifeboats were launched to join the search of the area, but it was soon clear that there were no survivors among the two pilots and one passenger aboard the two Gazelles. The pilot of XX415, Ft-Lt Robert Howley, whose award of the AFC had been announced in the Jubilee Honours list only two days earlier, was on a two-year exchange posting and joined the team at the beginning of the season. His passenger was Lt-Com. Geoffrey Bailey. The pilot of XW859 was Lt Paul Brown. All three were killed on impact.

The wreckage of the two Gazelles was located and recovered within days of the accident and during the subsequent technical investigation no evidence of any pre-accident malfunction was found in either aircraft.

This accident was untypical of most Royal Nay rotary-wing accidents, since it occurred when six helicopters were practicing aerobatic manoeuvres in very close formation at low level. Although all members of the team were highly experienced pilots, there remained little margin for error.

However, despite the fact that the team missed the remainder of the 1977 season, the Sharks reappeared the following year, now a four-aircraft team, and continued to entertain countless thousands at some twenty air displays up and down the country for the next fourteen years without mishap. The team's four Gazelles were flown by No. 705 NAS QHIs, who practised and performed in their spare time, invariably before or after their normal working day. Since 1987 the squadron supported a second display team, the 'Pussers Pair', which featured two Gazelles that took part in ten displays each season, again flown by regular instructors.

One of the RN Gazelle display pilots was Michael Greenland:

Selected to be a QHI, or 'Beefer', in 1989, I returned to the Gazelle HT.2 to refresh and then complete the QHI course with CFS(H) on the HT.3 at RAF Shawbury. Qualifying as a B2 I started my first QHI tour at No. 705 NAS in November 1989.

My first year on the squadron was predominately taken up with gaining my QHI skills and re-categorising from probationary B2 to a B1 instructor, so no time for displaying! Among the twenty-four-odd staff, there was significant competition to become a member of the Sharks Display team. I was fortunate to be selected for one of two solo display pilots for the 1991 season.

Work up started in January with Lt Kevin Mathieson RN, an experienced QHI and display pilot. The key manoeuvres to practice, which were not part of the basic helicopter training syllabus, were Advanced Wing Overs and Pedal Turns. Essentially up to 90 degrees nose up and 90 degrees of bank while maintaining positive g. Having mastered these it was a case of stitching it altogether in a coherent short display that showed off the key aspects of a helicopter, such as Fast Stops/Quick Stops, hovering manoeuvres and so forth. The trick, at the time, was to make it look, to the more casual observer, as if you were turning the Gazelle upside down, even if you weren't! Also it was being able to adjust your display for a relatively small field size area and, in the event of low visibility and cloud base do something airborne so at least there was something flying and displaying if others, such as regular aircraft and parachutists, had had to abandon. The converse was equally true; I recall going to RIAT on a brilliant summer's day and wondering how to extend my display given the shear length of the display line!

After a final check out with the 705 NAS Senior Pilot, Lt Cdr Mark Osman RN, I was good to go. My first display was at home as part of a Wings Parade, so life seemed to have turned a full circle. However displaying in front of your super critical peers was a slightly daunting prospect, knowing the debrief that might follow!

All the displays were, varied, interesting and different in their own ways to very different audiences, be it at Rosyth Dockyard for a celebration, RAF St Athan for its annual air show, the Vale of White Horse county show in Oxfordshire or at the RN leadership School in HMS *Royal Arthur* in Corsham. I was also one of the RN entries competing with the Gazelle in the annual British Helicopter Championships. So in all 1991 was a busy year, during which I passed the significant milestone of 2,000 rotary hours, the majority on the wonderful and brilliant Gazelle. My final display task was to display at Prestwick (HMS *Gannet*) and a flypast at HM Naval Base Faslane.

In 1992, the Sharks team was disbanded due to budgetary cuts but 705 NAS continued to provide a pair of Gazelles, simply known as the Gazelle Pair, up to 1996 when Gazelles were formally retired from the Royal Navy.

With the disbanding of 705 NAS at RNAS Culdrose in March 1997, a large number of its Gazelle HT.2s were placed in storage pending disposal. While some went to the RAF as instructional airframes, a few remained in use as 'hacks' for several Royal Navy units, including 847 NAS and Fleet Officer Naval Aviation at RNAS Yeovilton and the Naval Aircraft Repair Organisation at Fleetlands, while two remained is service with the Empire Test Pilots School (ETPS) in 2018.

Faced with lean budgets and an increasingly complex and dangerous defence and security environment at the turn of the century, QinetiQ and Northrop Grumman believed that they had identified a reliable, cost-effective Vertical Take-Off Unmanned Air System (VTUAS) capability that could form the basis for a radical change in the conduct of maritime patrol and war-fighting operations by the Royal Navy.

The recommended UK platform for the Fire Scout conversion, a tactical UAV based on the Schweizer 333 light helicopter that Northrop Grumman had developed for the US Navy, was the Gazelle. It was recognised that the Gazelle was a short-term solution, but it would have provided an extremely cost effective way for the Royal Navy to gain valuable, early operational experience with a VTUAS with a view to re-hosting the system in a more capable airframe as part of the Future Force 2020. The conversion of a Gazelle into a VTUAS platform was to have taken place at MOD Boscombe Down, while the flight test work for the demonstrator programme would be conducted at the QinetiQ West Wales UAV Centre. Conversion of the Gazelle to a UAS was offered for the Royal Navy RWUAS demonstration programme, but the AgustaWestland SW-4 SOLO was selected in the end and there was no ongoing plan to convert Gazelle into a UAS.

The first Royal Navy Gazelle HT.2, XW857, on a pre-delivery flight at Yeovil in 1973. (Leonardo)

One of the first batch of Gazelle HT.2s built in 1973, XW861 entered service with No. 705 Squadron at RNAS Culdrose. (Royal Navy)

RN No. 705 Squadron Gazelle HT.2 XW890 was one of the original members of the Sharks aerobatic team in 1977. (Royal Navy)

Gazelle HT.2 XX415 was one of the two Sharks aircraft that were lost in an accident on 13 June 1977. (Royal Navy)

A formation of nine Gazelle HT.2s used by the Royal Navy's helicopter display team, the Sharks, near Helston in Cornwall in 1976. (Royal Navy)

The Sharks display team was reformed with four Gazelle HT.2s from No. 705 Squadron in 1978. (Royal Navy)

Two No. 705 Squadron HT.2s belonged to the second Royal Navy display team, the Pussers Pair, which was formed in 1987. (Royal Navy)

Close aerobatic displays were highlighted by the four-ship Sharks team during the 1980s. (Alan Norris)

Above: A fly-past by the four Gazelle HT.2s of the Sharks display team at RNAS Culdrose in 1986. (Alan Norris)

Right: RN solo display pilots Lt Mike Greenland (left) and Lt Simon Langley (right) pose in front of their Sharks HT.2 in 1991. (Michael Greenland)

Pristine No. 705 Squadron HT.2 XW856 wearing the later large Sharks symbol on its tail at RNAS Culdrose in 1986. (Alan Norris)

HT.2 XX431 of Flag Officer Naval Aviation at RNAS Yeovilton took part in the 50th anniversary D-Day fly-past on 5 June 1994. (Crown Copyright)

Former No. 705 Squadron Gazelle HT.2 XW887 became a 'hack' with the Naval Aircraft Repair Organisation at Fleetlands in 1998. (Francois Prins)

CHAPTER SIX

Balkan Partizans

The Gazelle was also produced under licence by SOKO at Mostar in Yugoslavia and a total of 121 SA.341Hs and more than sixty-three SA.342Ls were built before production was curtailed in 1991 by the disintegration of the Federal Republic of Yugoslav. The first twenty SA.341H Gazelles were built by Sud Aviation in Marignane.

In Yugoslav People's Air Force and Air Defence (JRV i PVO) service they were known as Partizans and were designated by role: the HO-42 as the training/transport version of the SA.341H; the HO-45 as the training/transport version of the SA.342L; the HI-42 as the Hera scout version of the SA.341H; the HN-42M as the Gama attack version of the SA.341H; the HN-45M as the Gama 2 attack version of the SA.342L; and the HS-42 as the medevac version of the SA.341H.

The Gamas were armed with Soviet weapons, including four 9KL11 (9M14M) Malyutka, NATO designation AT-3 Sagger, wire-guided anti-tank missiles (ATMs) with the licence-built APX-334-02 Athos or the gyro-stabilised APX-334-25 sight and the laser rangefinder mounted above the cockpit, or two 9K32 (9M32M) Strela-2(M), NATO designation SA-7 Grail, air-to-air missiles (AAMs) used for the anti-helicopter missions.

Even as the desert dust was being washed off Coalition aircraft involved in the Gulf War, a new and potentially serious conflict was breaking out in Eastern Europe. On 28 June 1991 the Federal Republic of Yugoslavia was on the brink of a civil war. The Yugoslav republic of Slovenia declared independence two days earlier and Slovenian defence forces confronted the Yugoslav People's Army (JRV), which moved to protect international border posts. Fierce fighting on 27/29 June resulted in shooting down a helicopter on the outskirts of Ljubljana, the Slovenian capital. By 18 July the Yugoslav presidency decided to withdraw from Slovenian territory and Slovenia was granted its independence in 1992. The Slovenian Ten-Day War was only a prelude to a decade of conflict that resulted in the breakup of the Federal Republic of Yugoslavia. The Croatian War of Independence lasted from 1991 to 1995, the Bosnian War from 1992 to 1995, and the Kosovo War from 1998 to 1999, during which time a large number of Partizans were lost.

The Republic of Serbia, a constituent republic of Serbia and Montenegro, was formed in 1992. General Ratko Mladić, chief of staff of the Army of the Republic of Serbia in the Bosnian War of 1992–95, who was sentenced to life imprisonment for war crimes by the International Criminal Tribunal in 2017, was assigned HO-45 12882 as his personnel transport, piloted by Major Dusan Maran.

However, with Montenegro's secession from the union with Serbia in 2006, both became sovereign states in their own right. This led to the establishment of the Serbia Air Force and Air Defence (RV i PVO) with a much diminished inventory of aircraft and less than a third of the original number of Gazelle helicopters.

Serbia is now a member of the United Nations, the Organisation for Security & Co-operation in Europe and Partnership for Peace, and since 2014 the country has been negotiating its EU accession with perspective of joining the European Union by 2025.

The RV i PVO's Gazelle fleet in 2018 included forty-five SA.341H/SA.342L Gazelles for liaison and training, with the Hera reconnaissance and the Gama attack variants serving with the 204th Air Brigade's 890th Mixed Helicopter Squadron based at Batajnica near Belgrade and the 98th Air Brigade's 714th Anti-Armour Helicopter Squadron at Ladevci in central Serbia. An upgrade programme is underway that will feature a cockpit upgrade and a multi-sensor gimbaled turret above the cabin replacing the APX-334 gyro-stabilised sight. There are plans to integrate the new Advanced Light Attack System (ALAS) wire-guided missile with non-line-of-sight (NLOS) homing. Additionally, an imaging infrared (IR) seeker that transfers the guidance signal via fibre-optic cable is being designed for the Gazelle. The RV i PVO plans to keep the Partizan in service until 2030.

The Serbian Police's Helicopter Unit that provides aerial surveillance, border monitoring, VIP transport, medevac, and search and rescue. Based at Belgrade's Nikola Tesla Airport, the unit is equipped with four SOKO Gazelles, although only two are serviceable at a time.

In December 2016 the Ministry of Defence and the Ministry of Interior of the Republic of Serbia signed a contract with Airbus Helicopters for nine H145M helicopters – six for the RV i PVO and three for the Serbian Police. As part of the contract, Airbus Helicopters agreed to provide equipment and training, and certification went to the Moma Stanojlović Aviation Institute at Batajnica in Belgrade as the maintenance centre for air force and police Gazelle helicopters, and to include the institute into the Airbus Helicopters repair network.

Another eleven SOKO-manufactured Gazelles are operated by the Air Force Brigade of Bosnia and Herzegovina at Banja Luka. These regularly take part in Euro-Atlantic Disaster Response Coordination Centre (EADRCC) exercises, which is NATO's principal civil emergency response mechanism in Europe. Montenegro became the twenty-ninth member of NATO in June 2017 and its air force operates fourteen Partizan helicopters, which are based at Podgorica.

SOKO-built Yugoslav People's Air Force and Air Defence service SA.341H 12708, a HI-42 Hera scout version of the Partizan.

The SOKO aircraft factory at Mostar in former Yugoslavia produced more than 180 Gazelle helicopters from 1973 to 1991.

SOKO HO-42 12666, a training and transport version of the Partizan, is seen in early Serbian Air Force markings at Tivat in 2002. (David Oliver)

A Serbian Air Force SA.341H Partizan landing at Tivat Airport during a military display in September 2002. (David Oliver)

A close formation
of Serbian Air Force
HN-45M Gama 2
attack versions of the
SA.342L Partizan.
(Dimitrije Ostojic)

A sniper riding on
the skid of a Serbian
Air Force of a HO-45
Hera Partizan 12879
in October 2009.
(Dimitrije Ostojic)

SOKO HN-45M Gama 2 Partizan 12912 flying over Belgrade during the 2012 Batajnica Air Show. (Dimitrije Ostojic)

Serbian Air Force HN-45M Gama 2 Partizan firing an AT-3 Sagger wire-guided anti-tank missile during a live firing exercise in 2012. (Dimitrije Ostojic)

A pair of Serbian Air Force HN-42N Gama Partizans, 12806 and 12820, in April 2013. (Dimitrije Ostojic)

71

Serbian Police SOKO SA.342L1 YU-HFF and SOKO ΛS.342J YU-HEΛ overflying Belgrade during a police demonstration in 2017. (Serbian Police)

A Serbian Police SOKO Partizan armed with a 20-mm cannon. (Serbian Police)

Serbian Police SA.342J YU-HEA and SA.342L1 YU-HEC offload special police forces at a joint strike demonstration in April 2018. (Serbian Police)

A doorless Montenegrin Special Forces HS-42 Partizan, 12752, flies low during in the Danilovgrad Training Center in Montenegro in December 2006. (US Army/ Jim Greenhill)

An immaculate Montenegro Air Force HO-42 Partizan, 12667, undergoing maintenance at Podgorica. (MAF)

An Air Force Brigade of Bosnia and Herzegovina SOKO Partizan undertaking a MEDEVAC role during a NATO emergency response exercise in September 2017. (NATO)

CHAPTER SEVEN

Worldwide Service

More than half of the Gazelles produced were exported to twenty-one countries, the majority of them in North Africa and the Middle East, where more than 200 remained in service in 2018.

When first flown on 11 May 1973 the uprated 'hot and dry' SA.342K variant secured initial sales for twenty aircraft to Kuwait for use in attack and observation roles. Three Kuwait Air Force SA.342Ks were lost during the first Gulf War while eight escaped to the Saudi Naval Air base at Jubail. Some thirteen surviving SA.342K Gazelles are currently operated by No. 33 Squadron, based at Ali Al Salem Airbase.

The second Middle East customer was Morocco, which obtained twenty-four SA.342Ks. During the Western Sahara War against the Polisaro Front in 1980 the Royal Morocco Air Force (RMAF) used Gazelles armed with Euromissile, later MBDA HOT wire-guided missiles to neutralise the Polisaro's T-54 and T-55 tanks and BMP armoured vehicles. The RMAF has a current fleet of twenty-two SA.342Ks based at Rabat-Salé, while the Royal Gendarmerie Air Squadron operates another three stretched SA.342L Gazelles.

The Tunisian Air Force operates a small fleet of SA.342L1 helicopters, five of which were upgraded by Aerotec Group in France in 2012, which included the installation of night sights. Also provided was NVG flight training for the Tunisian Air Force pilots.

The only non-Russian helicopter operated by the Syrian Arab Air Force (SAAF) was the SA.342L Gazelle, the first of fifty aircraft was delivered from France in 1977. The SAAF used HOT missiles against the Israelis during the 1982 Lebanon War (also known as Operation *Peace for Galilee*), with the Gazelle helicopters claiming at least thirty kills of Israeli armour, although several helicopters were lost during the conflict.

Since then Syria has been steadily building up the number of Gazelles in its fleet, which have seen considerable action during the six-year civil war. The defence of Al-Tabqa Airbase in 2014 saw the combat debut of the SA.342L Gazelle in the civil war which had been only used on a limited amount of reconnaissance missions until then. The open desert surrounding the airbase proved to be the perfect combat environment for these helicopters. Armed with HOT missiles, they saw heavy action against vehicles of the Islamic State.

However, due to the lack of spare parts and HOT missiles the Gazelles are now used predominantly in the VIP transport role, although pairs have regularly been observed patrolling the demilitarised zones. Videos have been released showing the shooting down of at least two Syrian Arab Air Force Gazelles by rebel forces with TOW anti-tank missiles. Around forty SA.342Ls were still believed to be operational with No. 976 Squadron, based at Mezze, in 2018, with a few helicopters permanently detached to other airbases.

Iraq obtained some forty plus SA.342L Gazelles from France, which was one of Iraq's major arms suppliers in the 1970s. Iraq employed HOT-armed Gazelles against Iranian armour during the Iran–Iraq War of 1980 to 1988, but they were only used sparingly during the 1991 Gulf War and suffered several losses at the hands of Coalition forces. The post-Saddam Iraqi Air Forces has acquired six former ALAT SA.342Ms refurbished by Aerotec Group in France, armed with 20-mm cannon operated by No. 88 Squadron at Al Taji Air Base.

Lebanon acquired eleven Gazelles – a mix of SA.341 and SA.342Ls – from France in 1980, but due to the civil war they saw little operational use and most were withdrawn. In 2007 the Lebanese Air Force received nine recently retired SA.342Ls, donated by the United Arab Emirates (UAE). Soon after their arrival they were in action when fighting broke out between Fatah al-Islam, an Islamist militant organisation, and the Lebanese Armed Forces in May 2007 in the Nahr al-Bared UNRWA Palestinian refugee camp. The Gazelles are currently operated by No. 8 Squadron at Rayak Air Base in the light attack role armed with HOT missiles, 12x68-mm SNEB or LAU-32 rocket pods, FN Herstal 12.7-mm machine gun pods and a GIAT Sabord 20-mm cannon.

The Qatar Emiri Air Force (QEAF) acquired fourteen SA.342L Gazelles between 1983 and 1985 on anti-armour attack and communications duties. The QAEF's No. 2 Rotary Wing currently maintains a fleet of ten SA.342Ls, which are operated by No. 6 (Close Support) Squadron based at Al Gharlyah Airbase at the Doha International Airport. In the paramilitary role two Westland-built SA.341 Gazelles were flown by the Qatar Police.

The largest Middle East operator of the Gazelle is Egypt, which acquired at total of 108 SA.342L/K Gazelles during the 1970s, the majority of which were locally assembled by the Arab British Helicopter Company (ABHCO) at Helwan. The British Arab Engine Company also produced the Turboméca Astazou engines for Egyptian-build Gazelles. More than sixty remain in service, mainly HOT anti-tank missile-armed SA.342Ks, with the Egyptian Air Force's 554th Tactical Helicopter Wing based at Kom Awshim and the Helicopter Training Brigade at El Minya.

Egyptian SA.342K Gazelle helicopters took part in the final combined live arms fire exercise at Mohamed Naguib Military Base during Exercise *Bright Star* in 2017, which is a combined command-post and field training exercise aimed at enhancing regional security and stability by responding to modern-day security scenarios with the Arab Republic of Egypt.

In June 1987, the Cyprus National Guard Air Command purchased a batch of six SA.342Ls armed with HOT-2 wire-guided ATMs, four of which were overhauled by Aerotec Group in 2014. The Gazelle remains in service with 450ME/1st Platoon at the Andreas Papandreou Air Base in the Paphos district.

Africa was another major market for the Gazelle. In the late 1970s the Rwandan Air Force was equipped and trained on French helicopters, including SA.342L Gazelles. However, during the civil war that raged from 1990 until 1994, its helicopter force and personnel suffered losses and were subsequently scattered. Only three Gazelles survived and they were seen together with two Mi-24s at Kigali International Airport in 1997. Two were later seen at Goma, in Zaire, in August 1997, already with provisional Congolese codes that indicated it is possible that up to five Gazelles were given to Kabila. A number of other Rwandan helicopters were seen in South Africa and Swaziland, indicating the involvement of South African companies and mercenaries in the Rwandan Civil War. A Gazelle was also seen being overhauled in Lanseria, South Africa.

Four SA.324L Gazelles are currently operated by the Rwandan Air Force, two by the Burundi National Army and three by the Gabon Armed Forces, and these have been refurbished by Airbus Helicopters Roumania.

Eight ex-ALAT SA.342Ms serve with the Angolan National Air Force and the Niger Air Force's three ex-ALAT SA.342F Gazelles were officially handed over in March 2013 at Base Aerienne 101 at Niamey. The aircraft were refurbished by Aerotech Group SAS in France prior to delivery and were armed with 20-mm cannons. French government-owned company DCI trained the Gazelle pilots and mechanics in France and Niger.

The Malawi Army Air Wing currently operates two ex-AAC Gazelle AH.1s supplied by the Paramount Group from South Africa in 2014. A further six ex-AAC AH.1s were acquired by the Paramount Group, which were sold to the Nigerian Air Force having been armed by Paramount with the Flexible Light Armaments System for Helicopters (FLASH) system that includes 12.7- and 20-mm machine gun/cannon pods and guided or unguided rockets and missiles.

As the only Far East Gazelle customer, China acquired eight SA.342L-1-armed Gazelles, which were the first dedicated attack helicopters to be operated by the People's Liberation Army Air Force (PLAAF). The purchase of further aircraft, including licensed production of the aircraft in China, had been under consideration, but this initiative was apparently abandoned following the end of the Cold War. The small fleet was used to develop anti-armour warfare tactics and the Gazelles have also been frequently used to simulate hostile forces during military training exercises.

One of the few South American Gazelle customers was Ecuador, which acquired a total of sixteen SA.342Ls in 1981. These were used by the Ecuadoran Army during the 1995 Cenepa War between Ecuador and neighbouring Peru, performing missions such as close air support of ground forces and escorting other helicopters. In 2008, a minor diplomatic dispute broke out between Colombia and Ecuador following a reportedly accidental incursion into Columbian airspace by an Ecuadoran Gazelle. Seven Gazelles remained in service with Grupo Aereo del Ejército No. 43 at Portoviejo in 2018 and the search for a replacement had begun. Apart from France and the UK, Ireland was the only other European operator of the Gazelle. Irish Air Corps Helicopter School operated a pair of SA.342L Gazelles mainly for helicopter training, or more specifically for conversion of pilots from fixed-wing to rotary-wing. The type was also used for instrument flying training and a limited amount of VIP transport. The Gazelles were equipped with VOR, ILS and ADF to enable full helicopter IFR training to be given on the type. They were withdrawn from service in December 2005.

Kuwait Air Force SA.342K Gazelles KAF-502 and KAF-514 wearing Gulf War stripes around the tail boom. (KAF)

Kuwait Air Force SA.342K Gazelles over the battleground following the withdrawal of Iraqi forces during Operation *Desert Storm* in February 1991. (KAF)

Royal Moroccan Air Force SA.342L CN-ACC over Menara Air Base, Marrakech, in April 2012. (Peter Foster)

A Tunisian Air Force SA.342L1 operated by No. 32 Squadron taking part in a desert exercise. (TAF)

One of Morocco's Royal Gendarmerie Air Squadron's three stretched SA.342L Gazelles is seen at Tangier in 2007.

A Syrian Arab Air Force SA.342L captured by Israeli forces during the 1982 Lebanon War. It is now displayed at the Israeli Air Force Museum at Hatzerim. (Wikipedia)

HOT-armed Syrian Arab Air Force SA.342L Gazelles have been deployed to desert locations during the recent civil war. (SAAF)

This Syrian Air Force SA.342L Gazelle, armed with four HOT ATMs, is based at Mezze. (SAAF)

An Iraq Air Force SA.342M Gazelle in the Iraqi Army Aviation Command's newest maintenance hangar at Taji in January 2011. (USAF)

Former UAE SA.342L Gazelle L816 is operated by the Lebanese Air Force's No. 8 Squadron at Rayak Air Base in the light attack role. (David Oliver)

One of the large number of SA.342K Gazelles assembled by the Arab British Helicopter Company in the 1970s remain is Egyptian Air Force service. (USAF)

Two Egyptian Air Force SA.342K Gazelles taking part in a live-fire exercise during *Bright Star* 2017 at Mohamed Naguib Military Base. (USAF)

The Cyprus National Guard Air Command's HOT-2 armed SA.342L1 352 at Andreas Papandreou Air Base in October 2008.

Gabon Armed Forces' SA.342L Gazelles were refurbished by Airbus Helicopter Romania in 2014. (Airbus Helicopters)

One of Niger Air Force's three ex-ALAT SA.342F Gazelles, which were handed over in March 2013, are seen at Base Aerienne 101 at Niamey, having been refurbished by the Aerotech Group.

One of eight SA.342L Gazelles acquired by the PLAAF in the 1980s that are used to develop anti-armour warfare tactics.

A total of sixteen HOT-armed SA.342L Gazelles were delivered to the Ecuadorian Army in the early 1980s. (Peter Foster)

Left: Based at Portoviejo, the Ecuadoran Army's SA.342L fleet are being withdrawn from service with no replacement selected. (Peter Foster)

Below: The Irish Air Corps operated a pair of SA.342L Gazelles in training and communications roles until 2005. (IAC)

CHAPTER EIGHT

Civilised Gazelles

With production of military variants of the Gazelle underway at Marignane and Yeovil, a civil version, the SA.341G, was launched. Powered by the Astazou IIIA turboshaft, it gained French Secretary General for Civil Aviation (SGAC) certification on 7 June 1972 and US Federal Aviation Administration (FAA) certification on 18 September. In January 1975, it was announced that the SA.341G had become the first helicopter in the world to be authorised to be flown by a single pilot under IFR Cat.I conditions.

It was subsequently certified for IFR Cat.II operation, with a ceiling of 100 feet (30 metres) and 1,200 feet (365 metres) forward visibility. Equipment fitted to the aircraft that qualified for the FAA certification comprised a Sperry flight director coupled to SFENA, later Sextant Avionique, servo dampers.

In addition to the standard SA.341G, a stretched version was offered that had the rear portion of the cabin modified to provide an additional 8 inches (20 cm) of legroom for the rear seat passengers.

Another variant for commercial operators, the SA.324J, was similar to the military SA.342L. With an improved Fenestron tail rotor, it had a higher maximum take-off weight. It was certified by the DGAC on 27 April 1976 and deliveries began a year later, although only fourteen were built at Marignane.

Experienced civil helicopter pilot instructor and editor of *Helicopter Life*, Georgina Hunter-Jones has fond memories of the Gazelle:

It had a really good starting system, especially given the era in which it was built. It was very simple to start, just a couple of switches and then the engine started. You could also separate the engine and the blades, so keep the engine running while stopping the blades. This, I imagine, was a necessary military thing in case you want to pick up passengers, but were in a place when it would not be sensible to shut off the motor. This compares well with machines of the period, such as the Bell 206 Jet Ranger, which were prone to hot and hung starts having a rather more complex starting system. I also remember that there was a door jettison switch, which, while clearly useful for the military, it had to be wire locked in for civilian use as passengers were prone to accidentally jettisoning the door and causing damage and cost.

It had fully hydraulic controls, which made it super sensitive and wonderful to fly. It was extremely fast and felt rather like a sports car compared to the Jet Ranger, which had more of a saloon car feel. I remember doing quite a lot of diving down and pulling up fast into torque turns etc., which were extremely nimble. No surprise then that it is used for aerobatics! It was quite hard to slow down when coming in to land as the body was so sleek.

The Fenestron tail meant that the pedals were very effective and then at moments in the arc less so, and thus quite different from the standard tail rotor machines I was used to flying. It was quite easy to put the machine out of balance, and then harder to get it back into balance. I believe that the early Gazelles had a problem with the stators on the tail, which were replaced because there were problems with wind in a certain direction. The Gazelle I flew also had a useful Stability Augmentation System (SAS).

With only small numbers of civil Gazelles produced, currently those on the civil registers of more than a dozen countries, including Russia and the United States, are former military helicopters, the majority of which are Westland-built ex-AAC, RAF and RN versions and SOKO-built Partizans.

Gazelles were used in several Hollywood films, including *Gauntlet*, which featured a dramatic air chase, ending in the helicopter crashing. For the 1984 film *Blue Thunder*, two SA.341G Gazelles were purchased from Aérospatiale by Columbia Pictures for $190,000 each and were flown to Cinema Air in Carlsbad, California, where they were heavily modified into winged-gunships for the film.

Apart from privately owned and operated Gazelles, they have also been used for training helicopter pilot by flying schools, the most notorious being Specialist Flying Training (SFT), based at Carlisle Airport, which operated a fleet of eight SA.341Gs in the 1980s. It offered a 60-hour basic course and a 115-hour advanced course on the Gazelle to meet the helicopter flying training of foreign military customers – one of which was Iraq.

With the blessing of International Military Services Ltd – the British government-owned company that liaised between foreign governments and British commercial companies – SFT signed a contract to train twenty-five Iraqi pilots in 1983. The school's flying syllabus was devised for the Iraqi government by SFT's ex-RAF chief flying instructor.

The Iraqi students had limited experience of low-level training and after one of them was involved in a fatal accident in an SFT Jet Ranger, all helicopter training was subsequently conducted on the more robust Gazelle. At the end of the courses the Iraqi government was pleased with the results and wanted to continue the arrangement, but difficulties with financing the contract led SFT to cease military training.

On qualification, SFT trained pilots returned to Iraq with the rank of second lieutenants to begin operational training, some of whom subsequently served with British Forces during the first Gulf War in 1991.

One of SFT's SA.341Gs, G-SFTG, was sold in 1986 to a private owner, with whom it was re-registered G-RALE. In August 1988, the police learned that a helicopter had flown from the continent and was about to drop off drugs in Harewood Forest near Andover. The helicopter was G-RALE and it was intercepted by an RAF Puma, which chased the Gazelle to Hurn, where the pilot landed on the A303 and gave himself up to face a five-year jail sentence. The Gazelle was impounded and later sold. It is currently registered G-GAZA.

A more rewarding role, but no less demanding, is the Gazalle's anti-poaching operations in Africa. In 2013 a former AAC AH.1 was donated by the Ichikowitz Family Foundation in association with the Paramount Group – South Africa's largest private aerospace and defence group – to South African National Parks to fight rhino poachers in Kruger National Park, South Africa's largest game reserve. A second former Royal Navy HT.2 Gazelle, registered ZU-HBH, was donated in 2015. The Paramount Group Anti-Poaching and K9 Academy houses one of the largest K9 breeding and training facilities in Africa. Specialising in anti-poaching activities, it provides combat training courses for park rangers and rapid response unit training for K9 teams, including rappelling from helicopters for fast deployment.

In September 2016 the Ichikowitz Family Foundation donated another Gazelle helicopter and specialised anti-poaching dogs to the Gabon National Parks Agency to set up an Anti-Poaching Rapid Response Task Force. This helicopter was one of a number of ex-AAC Gazelle AH.1s acquired by the Paramount Group, which refurbished it and equipped it for its new anti-poaching role.

In the United Kingdom the Gazelle Squadron Display Team that was established in 2014 currently perform as a two-aircraft flying display and provide additional aircraft for static display at air shows across the country. The squadron consists of around thirty-five volunteers, who supply their time and skills throughout the year to operate and maintain the fleet of nine former military Westland Gazelle helicopters from the AAC, RN, RAF and Royal Marines, which are painted in colour schemes to accurately reflect the fifty years of military service by the Gazelle with the British Armed Forces. Based at its private airfield near Hurstbourne Tarrant in Hampshire, all of the squadron's personnel are civilian and many are experienced former military pilots, engineers and ground crew, most of whom performed with the AAC Eagles and RN Sharks display teams.

The numbers of civil registered Gazelles worldwide are expected to multiply when the ALAT and Army Air Corps fleets are withdrawn from service as this remarkably capable and resilient helicopter approaches its 60th anniversary.

SA.341G Gazelle C-GUMH, belonging to Heli Voyageur at Val d'Or in Quebec, is seen in 1970. (Aviafora)

Polizei Niedersachs' SA.342J Gazelle D-HOPP in 1973. (David Oliver)

SA.341G F-GETS belonging to the French helicopter charter company MTS at Avignon Airport in June 1986. (David Oliver)

SA.341G G-SFTC, one of Specialist Flying Training's fleet of nine Gazelles, at Carlisle Airport in 1984. It is currently registered G-LOYD. (David Oliver)

An Iraqi student pilot during a training flight in an SFT Gazelle at Carlisle Airport in 1984. (David Oliver)

SA.341G G-SFTG, seen heading a line-up of SFT Gazelles at Carlisle Airport in 1984, was later intercepted while drug running in 1988. (David Oliver)

89

G-GAZA, formerly registered G-SFTG and later registered G-RALE, was impounded in 1988 after a failed drug-running flight. (Peter Olding)

SA.341G G-BKLV of Helicopter Services Limited is seen fitted with floatation gear at Castle Ashby in 1985. (Alan Norris)

SA.341Gs G-GZLE (ex-G-SFTD) and G-UZEL are seen on the Solent Fort's helipad in 2003. (Georgina Hunter-Jones)

SA.341G G-BAGL, seen at Elstree Airport in 1997, was previously a Westland Helicopters demonstrator aircraft. (David Oliver)

The second production Westland SA.341G Gazelle, built in 1972, is currently on the Serbian register as YU-HHS. (David Oliver)

SOKO-built SA.342H HO-42 Partizan, registered YU-HEI, seen at Elstree Airport in 1999, has since been withdrawn from use. (David Oliver)

Hungarian registered, SOKO-built SA.341H HA-PPY is seen at Duxford in 2005. (Alan Norris)

One of the few Aérospatiale SA.341Js built, HA-LFH is seen at Wycombe Air Park in June 2014. (David Oliver)

Former AAC Gazelle AH.1 XX432, built in 1975, is currently owned by Falcon Aviation Ltd and is registered G-CDNO. (Gazelle Squadron)

Westland SA.341B Gazelle AH.1 XW885 first flew in November 1973. Now registered G-ZZEL, it currently serves with the Gazelle Squadron. (Gazelle Squadron)

Westland SA.342C XW853 was the first HT.2 delivered to the Royal Navy in 1974 and is currently registered G-IBNH. (Gazelle Squadron)

Formerly Irish Air Corps SA.342L Gazelle 241, HA-LFQ gained its Hungarian civil register on 2007. (Alan Norris)

Formerly AAC AH.1 XZ299, RA-05703 is currently one of more than twenty Gazelles on the Russian civil register. (Vitaly)

Stretched SA.342J F-HGUN wearing an ALAT colour scheme departing Courchevel in the French Alps in March 2014. (Gilles Paccalet)

Aérospatiale SA.342G Gazelle N341GG is based in Europe and participated in the Gazelle 50 Fly-In at Middle Wallop on 8 April 2017. (Aviafora)

Gazelle AH.1 ZB688 was registered G-CHMF in 2009. It was later donated by the Ichikowitz Family Foundation to the South African National Park's Anti-Poaching Unit. (Aviafora)

Formerly of the Royal Navy, Gazelle HT.2 ZU-HBH is the backdrop to the Paramount Group's Anti-Poaching and K9 Academy demonstration in South Africa. (Paramount Group)

A K9 anti-poaching team prepare to drop from Paramount's SA.341C Gazelle ZU-HBH in South Africa's Kruger National Park. (Paramount Group)

In 2016 the Ichikowitz Family Foundation donated another AH.1 Gazelle to the Gabon National Parks Agency to set up an Anti-Poaching Rapid Response Task Force. (Paramount Group)

Two of the Gazelle Squadron's immaculate Gazelles, HT.3 ZB627/G-CBSK and HT.2 XX436/G-ZZLE. (Gazelle Squadron)

The Gazelle Squadron's HT.2 XX436/G-ZZLE is in temporary 3 CBAS Royal Marines colours when seen at Wycombe Air Park in 2014. (David Oliver)